Drafting Commercial Contracts

Legal English Dictionary and Exercise Book

MICHAEL HOWARD

Drafting Commercial Contracts

Copyright © 2015 Michael Howard

All rights reserved.

ISBN: 1514273292
ISBN-13: 978-1514273296

Drafting Commercial Contracts

License Notes

This book is licensed for your personal enjoyment only. This book may not be re-sold.

Drafting Commercial Contracts

Drafting Commercial Contracts

CONTENTS

Dictionary

1	Types of Contracts	1
2	Commercial Considerations	7
3	Introductory Contract Terms	17
4	Duties and Obligations	25
5	Boilerplate Clauses	33
6	Glossary	37

Exercises

7	True or False	47
8	Vocabulary Gap Fill	51
9	Preposition Gap Fill	55
10	Collocation Gap Fill	59
11	Replace the Incorrect Word	63
12	Answers	67

Drafting Commercial Contracts

BUY MORE TITLES AT:

http://www.legalenglishbookstore.com

DICTIONARY

1 TYPES OF CONTRACTS

Agency Agreement (noun): An agency agreement is an arrangement between two parties where one party (the "principal") asks another party (the "agent") to represent them and create contractual legal relationships with a third party. This means that the agent has authority to make decisions for the principal and will negotiate directly with the third party. Agency agreements are very common and are used for marketing, distribution, customer support and many other types of contracts. For example, Company A (the principal) manufactures cars in Japan. Company A authorises company B (the agent) to advertise the car in Brazil. Company B negotiates and contracts with television company C (the third party) to show a number of TV advertisements for the car in Brazil. In this example, there will be an agency agreement between company A and company B for company B to represent company A in the contract negotiations with company C.
Associated Words: Agent (noun), Distribution (Noun), Marketing (noun), Principal (noun), Third Party (noun).

Consumer Credit Agreement (noun): This is a contract where a third party (usually a bank) agrees to finance the purchase of the goods or services. This contract is separate from the contract between the buyer and seller.
Associated Words: Goods (noun), To Purchase (verb), Third Party (noun).

Distance Selling (noun): A distance selling contract is a contract, which is performed without the parties meeting face to face. Examples of distance selling contracts are internet sales, catalogue sales, sales via telephone, sales by email and sales by fax. There are specific regulations for these types of contracts to ensure that the consumer is given the same rights and

protection as a consumer would if they entered the contract face to face with the seller.
Associated Words: Consumer (noun), Seller (noun), Rights (noun).

Distribution Agreement (noun): A distribution agreement is a contract between a manufacturer of goods and a third party. The third party is responsible for marketing and distributing the goods. Usually, under a distribution agreement, the third party will market and sell the goods using their own name. One important difference between a distribution agreement and an agency agreement is that under a distribution agreement title and ownership of the goods will usually pass to the third party (and so does the risk). Under an agency agreement the title and ownership of the goods remains with the manufacturer until the goods are sold to the final buyer.
Associated Words: Agency Agreement (noun), Marketing (noun), Risk (noun), Third Party (noun), Title to Goods (noun).

E-commerce (noun): This is a general term for trading and commercial contracts entered into over the internet. There are special considerations when entering into such contracts such as data protection and secure payment methods.
Associated Words: Data Protection (noun), To Enter Into (phrasal verb).

Franchise (noun): This is a type of agreement where a company (A) grants a licence to another company (B) to sell, manufacture or distribute company A's products. Company B will usually use company A's method, trademarks and technology and will be paid a royalty or commission from the profit. For example, company A is a well-known fast-food restaurant chain and wants to expand its network of restaurants. They can enter into franchise agreements with other independent companies who will run the restaurants (or "franchises") in exactly the same way as the original restaurants, using all the same methods and trademarks. This agreement is very useful for well-known brands with well-established trademarks and reputation who wish to expand their business.
Associated Words: Commission (noun), To Grant (verb), Licence (noun), Profit (noun), Trademark (noun).

To Hire (verb): This verb means paying money to borrow something from someone or to use a product or service temporarily. To hire is commonly used in relation to hiring goods such as cars, bicycles, boats, etc. A hire-purchase agreement is a contract where the goods or services for hire become permanently owned by the buyer after all payments have been made to the seller.
Associated Words: Hire Agreement (noun), Hire Purchase Agreement (noun).

Hire Agreement (noun): This is a contract between a person (the "Hirer") who pays to use a product or service for a period of time. This type of contract is used between a hirer and an owner when the owner loans its goods to the hirer for use without an option to purchase them.
Associated Words: To Hire (verb), Hirer (noun), To Loan (verb), To Purchase (verb).

Hire-Purchase Agreements (noun): This agreement is similar to a hire agreement but the hirer has the option to purchase the goods after a period of time, or after a certain amount of the loan has been re-paid.
Associated Words: To Hire (verb), To Loan (verb), Option (noun), To Purchase (verb).

Insurance (noun): An insurance agreement is an agreement between an insurance company (the "insurer") and a customer (the "insured"). The insured pays a premium, for example every month, so that in the future the insurer will compensate the insured for any loss suffered which is covered by the insurance agreement. There are many difference types of insurance agreement and each type has very specific conditions that the insured must meet in order for the insurer to compensate the loss suffered. The terms of the agreement are set out in a long document called an insurance policy.
Associated Words: To Insure (verb), Insured (noun), Insurer (noun), To Compensate (verb), Conditions (noun), Loss (noun), To Set Out (verb). To Suffer (verb).

Lease (noun): This is a very popular type of agreement that permits a party to use property, land, vehicles or a piece of equipment for a period of time. Under a lease agreement ownership and legal title remains with the owner.
Associated Word: Title (noun).

To License (verb): This verb means to give permission to use something for a period of time. A person who gives permission or a license is called a "licensor" and the receiver is called a "licensee". A common example of the verb would be in intellectual property law where copyright or patents are sometimes licensed between licensors and licensees. The contract is referred to as a Licence Agreement. An important aspect of a licence agreement is that legal title will remain with the licensor. In British English the noun of the verb is spelt "licence", while in American English is it spelt "license".
Associated Words: Licence (British English noun), License (American English noun), Licensee (noun), Licensor (noun).

Loan Agreement (noun): This is a very common commercial contract between a creditor (for example, a bank) and a debtor. A loan agreement is a contract where the debtor will borrow money from the creditor and agrees to pay the money back, usually in instalments, plus interest for an agreed period of time.
Associated Words: To Loan (verb), To Borrow (verb), Creditor (noun), Debtor (noun), Instalments (noun), Interest (noun).

Marketing (noun): This is an agreement for one party to conduct the promotion and advertising of goods or services for the manufacturer or seller.
Associated Word: Goods (noun).

Outsourcing (noun): To outsource means to transfer the duties and obligations of delivering a service to an external provider. This external provider will then provide the service. Common outsourcing agreements used by businesses are for IT services, telephone call centres and basic office administration. For example, it is common for global banks to outsource their telephone banking services to countries with lower costs. Outsourcing agreements are more complex than straightforward contracts for the supply of goods or services as they often involve the transfer of people, assets and contracts.
Associated Words: To Outsource (verb), Outsourced (adjective), Assets (noun), Duties and Obligations (collocation), Supply of Goods (collocation), Supply of Services (noun).

Sale of Goods (noun): This agreement governs the common contract between a buyer and seller. Goods is a general word for products or things for sale. Usually, these contracts will include conditions on price, term, termination, title, description, quality, quantity, exclusivity and dispute resolution.

Associated Words: Goods (noun), Conditions (noun), Exclusivity (noun), Quality (noun), Quantity (noun), Term (noun), Termination (noun), Title (noun).

Subrogation (noun): This is when a third party is given the rights or remedies of a claimant against a defendant. For example, Mr Smith takes out car insurance with LE Insurance Co Ltd. Mr Grim negligently crashes his car into Mr Smith's car causing £1,000 worth of damage. Mr Smith makes a claim with his insurance company to pay for the damage. Mr Smith also wants to issue a claim against Mr Grim for the £1,000. However, under the doctrine of subrogation, this right has been taken from Mr Smith by LE Insurance. LE Insurance may claim the £1,000 from Mr Grim but Mr Smith cannot. If Mr Smith also made this claim he would receive £1,000 from LE insurance and £1,000 from Mr Grim. This means that Mr Smith would receive compensation for the same loss twice (£2,000 in total). This is classed as unjust enrichment and is stopped by the doctrine of subrogation. Mr Smith may still have a claim against Mr Grim for any personal injury suffered. This is a different claim and so he would be free to issue a separate claim for it because this right was not subrogated to LE Insurance.

Associated Words: To Subrogate (verb), To Issue a Claim (collocation), Third Party (noun), Unjust Enrichment (noun).

Supply of Services (collocation): This is an agreement between one or more parties to provide a service in exchange for payment. Most agreements for a provision of a service are done in short form, however if the agreement is for a long term service then a more extensive agreement is required. Such an agreement needs to include terms and conditions for price, inflation, third party costs, employment and transport costs, customer changes to the service, development and improvement costs, term, termination, performance levels (the customer may want to set performance levels for the supplier using key performance indicators (KPIs), force majeure, remedies, quality of the services to be provided, exclusivity and dispute resolution.

Associated Words: Dispute Resolution (noun), Exclusivity (noun), Force Majeure (noun), Inflation (noun), Key Performance Indicators (noun), Price (noun), Term (noun), Termination (noun), Terms and Conditions (collocation), Third Party (noun).

2 COMMERCIAL CONSIDERATIONS

To Accept (verb): This verb is common in commercial contract law as it means that a party agrees to the terms and conditions of an agreement or contract is offered to them. It is the unconditional acceptance of the offer (without changing any of the terms) that forms the basis of a contract in law. There are other legal factors that must also be satisfied, for instance consideration, intention and authority to contract.
Associated Words: Accepted (past simple), Accepted (3rd form), Acceptance (noun), Authority to Contract (collocation), Consideration (noun), Party (noun), Terms and Conditions (collocation), (adjective).

To Affirm (verb): This verb means to say yes, to confirm or to answer in a positive way. In relation to commercial contracts, to affirm a contract means to confirm it is valid or enforceable.
Associated Words: To Enforce (verb), Valid (adjective).

To Amend (verb): This means to change. In legal English when a contract or document is changed or altered, the correct verb to use is to amend.

Authority to Contract (collocation): A party must have authority to enter into a legally binding contract. This means that they must have the right to sign the contract, either for themselves or for an organisation. It is very important that an individual has authority to contract because if they do not, the contract may not be legally binding. For example, for a company to

enter into a contract, it will be usually signed by one (or two) of the company directors. These directors must have the company's permission to sign contracts on behalf of the company. If they have the company's permission, then the directors have authority to contract.
Associated Words: To Bind (verb), To Enter into a Contract (collocation).

To Breach (verb): This is a very important word in legal English. It means that someone has broken an agreement or has not done something that they should have done. It is commonly used in commercial contracts, for example "breach of terms and conditions" or "breach of obligations".
Associated Words: Breached (past simple), Breached (3rd form), Breach (noun), Obligations (noun), Terms and Conditions (collocations).

Capacity to Contract (collocation): This phrase means that a party who signs a contract, intended to sign it and understands the terms and conditions that are stated in it. However, if a party does not have capacity to contract then it is not legally binding on that party. Common examples of parties who do not have capacity to contract are minors (children) and people who are mentally impaired or disabled. It is interesting to note that a contract that is in a different language to the party who signs it (and doesn't understand it) may still be legally bound by the contract.
Associated Words: To Bind (verb), Party (noun).

To Consent (verb): This means to allow or to permit something to be done or to happen.

Consideration (noun): This is necessary to form a legally binding contract and for a legal contract to be enforceable, it must have consideration. Consideration means that a transaction must take place and that both parties must receive something. In legal English, the phrase used is that consideration must be reciprocal. This means that consideration must travel both ways. The easiest example to use is the sale of goods. For example, Company X sells 10 television sets to Company Z for 5000 Euros. The consideration moving from Company X to Company Z is the 10 televisions. The consideration moving the other way is the 5000 Euros. In this transaction the consideration is reciprocal and has travelled both ways. This is called good consideration.
Associated Words: To Bind (verb), To Enforce (verb), Goods (noun).

Damages (noun): This is the legal English word for compensation or money paid by the liable party to the successful party. Please note that this noun is already plural and does not have a singular form. The noun "damage" means broken and is not a legal English term. Accordingly, the two words, damage and damages are completely different and should not be confused. Damages is a very important concept of civil litigation and this is the most common remedy awarded by the courts.
Associated Words: Liable (noun), Party (noun), Remedy (noun).

To Dispute (verb): This verb means to argue about something or to question something. It is used in legal English both as a verb and as a noun. The noun "dispute" is a situation when two or more people disagree about something. Civil litigation claims are also commonly called disputes.
Associated Words: Disputed (past simple), Disputed (3rd form), Dispute (noun), Disputed (adjective).

Duress (noun): The term "under duress" means that a person is being forced to do something that they do not want to do. It is similar in meaning to being put under pressure. In a legal English context it means that someone is forcing a party to sign or execute a contract that they do not want to sign. A party may be able to argue that a contract is not valid if they signed it "under duress". A similar phrase that is sometimes used is "undue influence".
Associated Words: Under Duress (collocation), To Execute (verb), Party (noun), Valid (noun).

To Enforce (verb): This means that the contract (or a clause in the contract) is legal and binding and can used or relied on in a court of law.
Associated Words: Enforced (past simple), Enforced (3rd form), Enforceable (adjective), To
Bind (verb), To Rely On (phrasal verb).

To Enter Into (phrasal verb): This verb is used in relation to negotiating or signing a contract. The phrase "to enter into negotiations" and "to enter into an agreement" are commonly used to describe the act of agreeing to negotiate or agreeing to contract with another party. For example, it is usual to hear sentences such as *"The contact was entered into on 6th September 2013"*.

Associated Words: Entered Into (past simple), Entered Into (3rd form), To Negotiate (verb).

To Expire (verb): This verb is used in legal English when a contract or time period ends. The context in which it is used is when such a contract or time period finishes naturally or without enforcement. The verb "to terminate" is also used in relation to the end of a contract.
Associated Words: Expired (past simple), Expired (3rd form), Expired (adjective), Expiry (noun), Expiration (noun), Termination (noun).

Frustration (noun): This means that a contract will be discharged because an event or situation caused the main duties and obligations of the contract to be impossible to be fulfilled. Examples of frustration are when it is impossible to fulfil obligations, that it is illegal to fulfil obligations or that the good or service is unavailable and so cannot be provided. For example, Mr Thomas hires a theatre to perform a music concert. Two days before the concert there is a storm and the theatre is flooded with water. It is impossible to perform the contract because of the doctrine of frustration.
Associated Words: To Frustrate (verb), To Discharge (verb), Duties and Obligations (collocation), To Fulfil (verb), To Hire (verb).

Heads of Terms (noun): This is a document that sets out the basic terms of a contract. It is commonly used for pre-contractual negotiations and to detail the terms that the parties think are the most important. Heads of Terms commonly include the main duties and obligations, for instance, applicable law, price, description, warranties, indemnities, exclusivity, dispute resolution and confidentiality. Heads of Terms are commonly used as a starting point for a first draft of a commercial contract.
Associated Words: Applicable Law (noun), Confidentiality (noun), Description (noun), Duties and Obligations (noun), Exclusivity (noun), Indemnity (noun), To Negotiate (verb), Party (noun), Pre-Contractual (noun), Price (noun), To Set Out (phrasal verb), Warranty (noun).

Injunction (noun): This is a type of remedy available from the court. An injunction is an order from the court that states that a party must do something or stop from doing something. A party who does not follow or obey an injunction can be liable in both criminal and civil law and can face serious penalties if they do not comply with the injunction.

Associated Word: Remedy (noun).

Intention (noun): This means that a party wants to contract with another party and enters into a contract knowing that they are entering into a legally binding situation. In legal English it is very important that all parties to the contract have the intention to contract.
Associated Words: To Intend (verb), Intended (past simple), Intended (3rd form), To Bind (verb), To Contract (verb), To Enter Into (collocation), Party (noun).

To Let (verb): This verb means that the owner of property, land, vehicles or pieces of equipment permits the hirer to use it for a period of time. It is important to understand the difference between the verb to rent and to let. For example, the landlord lets the property to the tenant. The tenant rents the property from the landlord.
Associated Words: Let (past simple), Let (3rd form), Landlord (noun), To Rent (verb), Tenant (noun).

Liquidated Damages (verb): Some contracts will state how much a party must pay if they are in breach of contract. This is called liquidated damages. In legal English there is a difference between liquidated damages and a penalty clause. Penalty clauses are not enforceable under English law and so for a liquidated damages clause to be valid the amount of the damages must be a genuine pre-estimate of loss.
Associated Words: Unliquidated Damages (noun), To Breach (verb), Damages (noun), To Enforce (verb), Loss (noun), Penalty Clause (noun), Valid (adjective).

Mitigation of Loss (collocation): This is a concept in common law that means that a person who has suffered loss must take reasonable action to stop or reduce any further loss or damage. If the defendant can establish in court that the claimant did not mitigate their loss, the court may reduce the award for damages to the claimant.
Associated Words: To Mitigate (verb), Damages (noun).

To Negotiate (verb): This verb means for two or more parties to discuss each parties positions with a view to agreeing a settlement, agreement or a contract. It is one of the most common verbs used in legal English as it is applied in all areas of law. Specifically, commercial contracts will always be negotiated between the parties and their legal representatives to agree a suitable compromise.

Associated Words: Negotiated (past simple), Negotiated (3rd form), Negotiation (noun), Compromise (noun), Party (noun), Settlement (noun).

To Offer (verb): This verb is the first step to enter into a contract with another party. To offer (or to make an offer) means to ask a party if they agree to exchange a good or service for something, usually money. If this offer is accepted by the other party then a basic contract is formed, depending on other legal factors being satisfied.

Associated Words: Offered (past simple), Offered (3rd form), Offer (noun), To Accept (verb), Party (noun).

Power of Attorney (noun): This means a document (or a person) which states that a person is legally entitled to enter into contracts or agreements on behalf of someone else. It is common for powers of attorney to be granted when one person is not physically or mentally able to enter into contracts themselves. In the UK is it common for solicitors to act as power of attorney on behalf of their clients.

Associated Words: To be Entitled To (collocation), To Enter Into (collocation).

Pre-Contractual (adjective): All discussions and negotiations that are made before contracts or agreements are signed are called pre-contractual. For instance, pre-contractual negotiations can continue for months before a contract is actually executed.

Associated Words: Pre-contract (noun), To Execute (verb), To Negotiate (verb).

Privity of Contract (collocation): This means that only a party to a contract may benefit from the rights in that contract and have duties and obligations imposed upon them. It means that the parties have privity of contract. There are also some situations in commercial contracts where third parties are also able to benefit from rights in a contract that they are not actually a party to.

Associated Words: Duties and Obligations (noun), Party (noun), Rights (noun), Third Party (noun).

Remedy (noun): This word is used to describe the way a court will try to compensate or resolve the harm or loss that the claimant has suffered. There are three main types of remedy common in commercial contract disputes. The most common remedy is damages. This is monetary compensation awarded to the claimant to compensate them for their loss. The second main type are called equitable remedies, such as an injunction or specific performance. These are court orders that specify that a particular action must be taken or is prohibited. The third main type are declaratory judgments which state the rights or legal relationships between parties.
Associated Words: To Remedy (verb), Damages (noun), Injunction (noun), Specific Performance (noun).

To Renew (verb): In legal English to renew is commonly used when a commercial contract is extended by all the parties on the same (or similar) terms as the original contract.
Associated Words: Renewed (past simple), Renewed (3rd form), Renewal (noun), Party (noun).

To Rent (verb): This means one party pays money to another to use a good or service for a period of time. Most commonly the verb rent is used in relation to property. For instance, "the company rents office premises from the local authority".
Associated Words: Rented (past simple), Rented (3rd form), Rent (noun), Goods (noun), Party (noun).

To Rescind (verb): This verb is used as a remedy to cancel a contract between parties. The principle of the remedy is to put all the parties back in the position they were in before they entered into the contract. Courts may have the power to rescind a contract in certain situations.
Associated Words: Rescinded (past simple), Rescinded (3rd form), Rescission (noun), Remedy (noun).

Restitution (noun): This is a type of remedy from the court commonly used with commercial contracts. Usually the court will order compensation to be paid by the defendant for the loss suffered by the claimant in the form of damages. However, in some situations the loss suffered by the claimant may be very small. The court has the option to order restitution. The law of restitution means that the court orders the defendant to pay any

profits that resulted from their breach of contract to the claimant. For example, Mr Burgess issues proceedings against Mr Shaw for breach of contract. Mr Burgess did not actually suffer any loss as a result of Mr Shaw's breach, but if Mr Shaw profited greatly from the result of his breach, then the court can order restitution and order that Mr Shaw pay his profits from his breach of contract to Mr Burgess.
Associated Words: Breach of Contract (collocation), Damages (noun), Remedy (noun).

Specific Performance (noun): This is a remedy from the court that orders a party to do a certain act. Usually specific performance is ordered to make a party fulfil their obligations under a contract. It is an alternative remedy when damages are perhaps not relevant to the claim as the claimant has not actually suffered any loss.
Associated Words: Damages (noun), Fulfil an Obligation (collocation), Remedy (noun).

To Take Instructions (collocation): This collocation is used between a lawyer and their client. It means that the client will tell the lawyer what they wish to do in relation to the legal matter. The lawyer will then be in a position to advise the client.

Uncertainty (noun): In commercial contracts, it is fundamental that the terms, conditions and meanings in the clauses are certain. A contract can be void because of uncertainty. This means that the contract may not be valid because the intentions of the parties or the meanings of the words cannot be interpreted with certainty.
Associated Words: Certainty (noun), To Interpret (verb), Terms and Conditions (collocation), Valid (adjective), Void (adjective).

Unfair Contract Terms (collocation): This collocation is very important in commercial contracts. It is a fundamental principle of consumer contract law that the contract must not be unfair on the consumer. This means that the terms and conditions in the contract must be reasonable and fair for all parties. There is significant statute and common law on what is fair and unfair in commercial contracts.
Associated Words: Consumer Contract (noun), Terms and Conditions (noun).

Unsolicited Goods (noun): These are goods or products that are delivered to someone who has not ordered them. In commercial contracts there may be terms that deal with the situation when goods have been delivered to parties who did not place an order for them. The parties can agree terms to decide in advance what should happen in this situation.
Associated Words: To Deliver (verb), Goods (noun), Party (noun), To Place an Order (collocation).

Valid (Adjective): In commercial contracts valid means that a contract is legally enforceable.
Associated Words: Validity (noun), Invalid (adjective), To Enforce (verb).

Drafting Commercial Contracts

3 INTRODUCTORY CONTRACT TERMS

To Accrue (verb): This means to increase. It is usually used in relation to interest on debts or money in arrears. For example, BigCo Inc. borrows $40,000 from Best Bank at an interest rate of 3%. The contract states that BigCo Inc. must pay instalments of $3,000 a month. BigCo Inc. is having financial problems and cannot pay $3,000 every month and so are now in arrears. The contract states that interest will accrue on the amount of money in arrears at a rate of 5%. The amount of money that is in arrears is accruing interest at a higher rate because BigCo Inc. are late with their instalment payments to Small Bank.
Associated Words: To Borrow (verb), Debt (noun), In Arrears (collocation), Interest (noun), Instalments (noun).

To Apply to (phrasal verb): This phrasal verb means that something relates or links to something else. For example, a commercial contract may state *"This contract applies to the provision of services in Germany only"*. This means that the contract only relates to the provision of services in Germany.
Associated Words: Provision (noun), Service (noun).

Business Day (noun): This means any day that is not a weekend or national holiday. For instance, Christmas Day and New Year's Day are not business days.

By/In Instalments (collocation): This phrase is used in commercial contracts in relation to payment. Payments made in/by instalments are payments that are not made in full but made on a regular basis in a smaller amount. It is common for goods to be paid for in/by instalments and these payments are usually detailed in a schedule at the back of the main contract.

Associated Word: Schedule (noun).

To Collect From (phrasal verb): This means to get something from someone else. For instance, a commercial contract may have a condition that the buyer must collect the goods from the seller at an agreed address.
Associated Word: Condition (noun).

Creditor (person or organisation): A creditor is a person or organisation who is owed money. For example, Mr Smalley borrows $5,000 from Big Bank. Big Bank is the creditor in this transaction because Mr Smalley owes them $5,000. Mr Smalley is called the debtor. In commercial contracts, the creditor may have certain rights connected with the money that they are owed by the debtor, especially if there is a charge on the debt.
Associated Words: Credit (noun), To Borrow (verb), Charge (noun), Debt (noun), Debtor (person or organisation), To Owe (verb).

To be Deemed (collocation): This phrase means to be seen or assumed. For example, if a contract states that the goods are to be deemed as received by the buyer by 27th June, then it means that the goods are seen or assumed as received by the buyer by 27th June. A commercial contract clause may state "The seller is deemed to have full legal title to the goods". This means that it is assumed that the seller is the full legal owner.
Associated Words: Clause (noun), Goods (noun), Title (noun).

Definitions (noun): This is a section of a commercial contract where the most important terms and phrases are explained in detail. The reason for a definitions section is to avoid misinterpretation or misunderstanding of the fundamental terms of the contract.
Associated Word: Terms (noun).

To Delay (verb): This verb means an event or situation happens later than previously planned.

Duties and Obligations (collocation): This term is one of the most common in commercial contracts. Duties and obligations are the tasks that must be done under the contract. The term means that each duty and obligation is extremely important for the contract to be fulfilled. For example, under a commercial contract for services, it will be a common

duty and obligation that the service provided is of a reasonable quality for the purposes required. Other duties and obligations will include payment, delivery of goods, time periods, quality of goods and services, etc. In legal English it is common to hear the phrase "to fulfil duties and obligations". This means to complete or finish them.
Associated Words: Delivery (noun), To Fulfil (verb), Goods (noun), Quality (noun), Services (noun).

Express Terms (noun): An express term is a clause or provision written in the contract. It is clearly stated in the contract and will usually include a duty or obligation to be fulfilled. These terms are specifically negotiated by the parties.
Associated Words: Clause (noun), Duties and Obligations (collocation), Implied Terms (noun).

To Execute (verb): This means to sign and date the contract to confirm all the parties agree to the terms and give the agreement a date.
Associated Words: Executed (past simple), Executed (3rd form), Party (noun).

Forthwith (noun): This means immediately, as soon as reasonably possible or without delay. Legal English has recently tried to move away from the old traditional "legalese" words, such as forthwith, and so any of the above alternatives are acceptable in drafting modern commercial contracts.
Associated Words: To Draft (verb), Legalese (noun).

From Time to Time (collocation): This phrase is commonly used in commercial contracts and means at any time.

Hereunder (noun): This is an old fashioned legalese word meaning somewhere below in this document.

Implied Terms (noun): These terms are not stated or written in the contract, but they still form part of the contractual duties and obligations. For example in sale of goods contracts there is an implied term that the goods must be of reasonable quality and fit for purpose.
Associated Words: Duties and Obligations (collocation), Goods (noun), Quality (noun).

In Arrears (collocation): In arrears means that you owe money that you should have paid before. This phrase is used to describe the situation when a buyer is late with their payments to the seller. For example, company X buys a boat from company Z and must pay company Z $1,200 per month in instalments for 5 years. If company X fails to pay any of the instalments, then it is in arrears. Another common example is when a person or company takes a loan out with a bank. If a person or company misses an instalment or a payment that they should have made, then their account will be in arrears. It is common for commercial contracts to contain a clause that the interest rate will increase on the amount of money that is in arrears.
Associated Words: Clause (noun), Interest (noun), Instalments (noun), Loan (noun), To Owe (verb).

In Respect of (collocation): This is a common phrase in commercial contracts which means connected with or to do with. For example, a clause in a commercial contract may state: *"Party B is to pay all outstanding invoices in respect of the delivered goods within 30 days of the date of delivery"*. This means that Party B must pay all outstanding invoices that are connected with the delivered goods within 30 days.
Associated Words: Clause (noun), To Deliver (verb), Goods (noun), Invoice (noun), Outstanding (noun).

Joint and Several Liability (collocation): This phrase means that if there is a group of two or more people who are liable for a debt, then all of the members of the group are liable individually and also together as a group. For example, if Mr and Mrs Benson are liable for damages under a commercial contract, the court may order that the liability is joint and several. This means that Mr Smith is liable for all of the debt, Mrs Smith is liable for all the debt, and together Mr and Mrs Smith are liable for the debt. The court can enforce the judgment against both Mr and Mrs Benson individually or together.
Associated Words: Damages (noun), To Enforce (verb).

To be Made on (phrasal verb): This phrasal verb is used in relation to the date of the contract. It is common to see the phrase *"This agreement is made on 17th February 2014"*. This means that the agreement was executed on this date.
Associated Words: Was Made On (past simple), To Execute (verb).

Neither Party (collocation): This term is used to suggest that if there are two parties to the agreement, then both parties do not have to do something. For example, a common clause may state *"Neither party is responsible for insuring the property"*. This means that both parties are not responsible for insuring the property.
Associated Words: Clause (noun), Insurance (noun).

Notwithstanding/Notwithstanding the Foregoing (noun): This is an old legalese word meaning despite or in spite of. The use of this term can complicate clauses and should be avoided from a drafting point of view. For example, older commercial contracts may include this term in some clauses, for instance "SmallCo is not permitted to consume alcohol on the premises. Notwithstanding the foregoing, SmallCo may hold private social events on the premises for up to a maximum of 20 people". The clause means that despite not being allowed alcohol on the property, the company may use the property for private social events for a small number of people.
Associated Words: Clause (noun). To Draft (verb), Premises (noun).

Outstanding (adjective): The word outstanding describes a situation when something is owed. It is usually used to describe a debt owed. In commercial contracts the word is commonly used in relation to money owed by one party to another. If the buyer owes the seller money, for instance for an unpaid invoice, then the buyer has an outstanding debt to the seller.
Associated Words: Debt (noun), Invoice (noun), To Owe (verb), Party (noun).

Penalty Clause (noun): A penalty clause states that in the event of a particular situation, an amount of money is to be paid as a penalty (for instance, breach of restrictive covenant). However, it is important to note that penalty clauses in commercial contracts can be unenforceable. The reason for this is that any attempt to estimate loss of a breach of a term or condition of the contract must be in relation to compensating the injured party, rather than punishing the party in breach. It is important to remember that when drafting commercial contracts (or negotiating them) that penalties for breaches of contracts may not be enforceable.
Associated Words: To Breach (verb), To Draft (verb), To Enforce (verb), Injured Party (noun), To Negotiate (verb).

Price (noun): This means the cost or the value of the goods or service provided in the contract. It is naturally, one of the most important terms and negotiating aspects of all commercial contracts.
Associated Words: Goods (noun), To Negotiate (verb), Service (noun), Terms (noun).

To Rely On/Upon (phrasal verb): In commercial contracts it is common for clauses to be "relied on or upon". For instance, a party will rely on representations made by another party to enter into the contract. In this commercial contracts context, the phrasal verb to rely on means to trust and depend on a representation or clause in an agreement.
Associated Words: Relied On/Upon (past simple), Relied On/Upon (3rd form), Clause (noun), Party (noun), Representation (noun).

Representations (noun): In legal English a representation is a factual statement made by a party that informs and persuades another party to enter into the contract. It is common for legal proceedings to arise because of representations (or "misrepresentations"). A misrepresentation is a factual statement that is later found to be false or a lie. In legal English is it common for a claim in tort for misrepresentation to be brought. For example, ABC Inc. and XYZ plc are negotiating over a contract for the supply of cars. ABC Inc. manufactures the cars and XYZ plc want to buy them from ABC and then sell them to customers. ABC make a representation to XYZ that all the cars were manufactured after 2010. There is no term in the contract about the age of the cars. XYZ buy the cars from ABC and later discover that they were all made in 2007. XYZ can bring a claim against ABC in tort for misrepresentation.
Associated Words: To Claim (verb), To Negotiate (verb), Tort (noun).

To Set Out (phrasal verb): This phrasal verb is very common in a commercial contract and means that something is stated or written somewhere else in the contract. For instance, a common clause is "The parties agree to fulfil all their duties and obligations as set out in this agreement". This means that the parties agree to complete their duties, which have been stated or written in full somewhere else in the contract.
Associated Words: Duties and Obligations (collocation), To Fulfil (verb).

Schedule (noun): This is a part of a contract usually found at the end or added as an appendix. Schedules are used to set out information that does not naturally fit into the main contract or agreement. For example, dates, prices, lists of products and other details are commonly added to contracts in the form of schedules.

Subject to (collocation): This collocation means that something will happen if something else happens also. For example, a clause in a contract may state *"the buyer agrees to purchase the goods subject to them being of a reasonable quality for their purpose"*. Here the collocation 'subject to' means that the purchase of the goods depends on them being of a reasonable quality for the purposes of their use.
Associated Words: Clause (noun), Goods (noun), To Purchase (verb), Quality (noun).

Sums Due (collocation): This means amount owed. For instance a commercial contract will usually state an exact date when payment must be made. Another way of saying this is that the sums are due on this date.
Associated Word: To Owe (verb).

To Supply (verb): This means to give or provide. It is one of the fundamental verbs used in commercial contracts for goods and services.
Associated Words: Supplied (past simple), Supplied (3rd form), Supply (noun), Supplier (person/organisation).

Term of Art (collocation): These are industry specific terms. Legal English has many terms of art which are specific to this industry and there will be many that are specific to commercial contracts. Examples of terms of art in commercial contracts are force majeure, boilerplate clause, warranties and guarantees.
Associated Words: Boilerplate Clause (noun), Force Majeure (noun), Guarantee (noun), Warranty (noun).

Thereof (noun): This is an old legalese word and means about something recently mentioned or said. For example, an old fashioned legalese clause may state *"The boxes will be delivered in excellent condition together with the contents thereof"*. The word thereof is talking about the contents of the boxes mentioned at the beginning of the clause.

Associated Words: Clause (noun), To Deliver (verb), Legalese (noun).

Time is of the Essence (collocation): This is a very common phrase in commercial contracts. It means that time is at the very centre of the contract and should be treated as one of the most important concepts. This has implications on the importance of delivery time, payment periods, etc. The phrase suggests that there will be serious consequences for breaches of terms and conditions that involve time.
Associated Words: To Breach (verb), Terms and Conditions (noun).

Under/At Clause (collocation): This means that a specific clause is referred to. For example, a client may ask their lawyer *"I don't understand the provisions under clause 5.3 in the contract"* or a lawyer may state *"Your client is in material breach of contract as they failed to pay the sums due under clause 3.4 of the contract"*. The phrase "under clause 3.4" means that this specific clause is being looked at or referred to.
Associated Words: Breach of Contract (noun), Clause (noun).

4 DUTIES AND OBLIGATIONS

All reasonable endeavours (collocation): Parties to a commercial contract should enter into the contract in good faith. This phrase states that a party (or parties) will do their best where reasonably possible. The phrase is used to make sure that a party fulfils a duty or obligation, or at least to use a reasonable amount of effort to fulfil them. This phrase is sometimes subject to negotiation as 'reasonable' is not a strong word in this situation. For instance, if you are asking another party to do something under the contract, then you would argue for the phrase 'all endeavours' or 'all best endeavours'. This is much stronger. However, if you are the party who must do something under the contract then you would argue that you should use 'all reasonable endeavours' as this obligation is easier to fulfil.

Associated Words: All Endeavours (collocation), All Best Endeavours (collocation), Duties and Obligations (collocation), Enter into a Contract (collocation), To Fulfil (verb), Good Faith (noun), Negotiation (noun), Party (noun).

Bill of Lading (noun): This is a type of contract used in shipping contracts. The contract is usually in the form of a receipt that the carrier of the goods (the ship) will give to the seller (or the agent of the seller) as evidence that the goods have been loaded and are being transported to the buyer. It is a legally binding document and can confirm the fulfilment of a contractual obligation. It can also be attached to the primary contract. The bill of lading can also confirm legal title of the goods, used as evidence for tax and insurance purposes and even include terms and conditions regarding quality and fitness for purpose. The receipt is also sent to the

buyer in order to guarantee payment when the goods are delivered.
Associated Words: To Bind (verb), To Deliver (verb), Fit for Purpose (collocation), To Fulfil (verb), Goods (noun), Guarantee (noun), Insurance (noun), Obligations (noun), Quality (noun), Terms and Conditions (noun), Title (noun).

Carriage by Sea (collocation): This is a legal English phrase commonly found in commercial contract that means that the goods subject to the contract are being transported by ship. This can have consequences in relation to insurance of the goods while they are being transported and this issue will also have to be dealt with in the contract.
Associated Words: Goods (noun), Insurance (noun).

Charter Party (noun): This is a type of commercial contract entered into between a ship-owner and a charterer. Under this contract, a ship is let or hired for the carriage of goods by sea on an agreed journey for a specific period of time.
Associated Words: Charterer (noun), Carriage by sea, Goods (noun), To Hire (verb), To Let (verb).

To Clear Funds (collocation): This means that payment for the goods or services has arrived in the bank account of the seller. Once the payment appears in the seller's bank account, the money has 'cleared'.
Associated Word: Goods (noun).

Commission (noun): This means that a person is paid a part or all of their salary as a percentage of the amount of goods that they sell. For instance, Mr Grant sells cars. He receives a basic salary plus 20% of the value of every car that he sells. This 20% is called commission.

Contingent Obligations (noun): This means that a duty or obligation is dependent on another event or situation happening first. For example, a contingent obligation may be if a buyer wishes to purchase more goods, then they can do so at the same price, if the buyer gives the seller two weeks notice. This is a typical example of a contingent obligation.
Associated Words: Goods (noun), Notice (noun), To Purchase (verb).

Data Protection (noun): This means that when a consumer purchases a good or service, the personal data and information given to the seller must be protected and kept confidential unless the buyer gives the seller permission to use the information given. This is common with distance selling and e-commerce commercial contracts as the buyer will usually give their email address and bank details to the seller over the internet. There may be clauses in commercial contracts that provide for the seller protecting the buyer's personal data.
Associated Words: Clause (noun), Distance selling (noun), E-commerce (noun), Goods (noun), To Purchase (verb).

To Default/To be In Default (collocation): This means that you failed to do something under the contract. For example, if the buyer does not pay an invoice on time then they are in default of the payment.
Associated Word: Invoice (noun)

Default Provisions (noun): Default provisions in commercial contracts are the situations that exist or will happen if the parties do not vary, change or alter them.
Associated Words: Provisions (noun), To Vary (verb).

Defective Product (noun): This means that products or goods are not of reasonable quality or not fit for their purpose. Commercial contracts usually contain a clause dealing with what the parties should do if a product is defective.
Associated Words: Clause (noun), Fit for Purpose (collocation), Goods (noun), Quality (noun).

Description (noun): In a commercial contract the good or service must be accurately described. This means that the seller must truthfully explain to the buyer what the product is or what the service will provide. The description of the good or service for sale is very important in commercial contracts because the buyer will rely on this when making a decision to enter into the contract. It is important that the seller is honest with the description because claims for misrepresentation can be brought if the buyer feels that the good or service was not as described in the contract.
Associated Words: To Describe (verb), To Enter Into (phrasal verb), Goods (noun), Misrepresentation (noun).

To Discharge (verb): This verb means to end the contract and for the parties to be free of their contractual obligations.
Associated Words: Obligation (noun), Party (noun).

Encumbrance (noun): This means a burden or restriction. It is commonly used in relation to property. For instance, if Company A wishes to buy a property to use as their offices, then then need to check that the land is free from all encumbrances. Encumbrances can include third party rights or charges that another party may have over the property.

Fair Wear and Tear (collocation): This phrase means that a product will usually become dirty, marked, scratched or damaged during its natural life. In commercial contracts there is usually a provision that states that fair wear and tear is normal and that it is a consequence of normal use. The phrase is used so that a buyer cannot bring a claim against the seller because the product becomes dirty or marked through normal everyday use.
Associated Word: Provision (noun).

Fit for Purpose (collocation): This means that the good or service for sale is suitable for the intended use of the good or service. This is connected to the concept that the good or service must be of a reasonable quality and this is usually an implied term of a commercial contract.
Associated Words: Goods (noun), Implied Term (noun).

To be Free from (phrasal verb): Commercial contracts usually contain a number of warranties, indemnities and guarantees. These can be in relation to one party confirming that the goods are in good condition and they are fit for purpose. Commercial contracts will usually use the phrase "to be free from" to draft a warranty or guarantee. For example, the buyer of goods will usually ask the seller to confirm that the goods *"are free from all encumbrances, defects and third party rights"*. This means that the goods are clean and without any problems or ownership issues. It is common for such language to be used when drafting warranties, indemnities and guarantees in commercial contracts.
Associated Words: Defective (adjective), Encumbrance (noun), Fit for purpose (collocation), Goods (noun), Guarantee (noun), Indemnity (noun), Warranty (noun).

Indemnity (noun): This is a term in a commercial contract that states that a party will pay an amount of money if a certain condition in the contract is not completed or later found to be not true. For example, if Company ABC want to buy Company DEF then Company ABC will ask Company DEF to grant them an indemnity for any tax liabilities that Company DEF owe to the tax authorities. This means that if Company DEF have any unpaid tax liabilities then Company DEF must indemnify Company ABC for the total amount of these tax liabilities.
Associated Words: Condition (noun), Party (noun).

Innominate Term (noun): This is a term in a commercial contract that is not a condition or a warranty.
Associated Words: Condition (noun), Warranty (noun).

In Relation to (collocation): This means that something is connected or linked to something else. For instance, it is common to see phrases such as *"The Buyer is relying on the warranty provided at clause 6.3 in relation to the condition of the goods"*. This means that the warranty at clause 6.3 is connected or discusses the condition of the goods. It is a very helpful phrase to connect one issue to another.
Associated Words: Clause (noun), Goods (noun), Warranty (noun).

Invoice (noun): This is a document used to detail the products, goods or services that have been ordered by the buyer. Usually, payment details are also set out in an invoice.
Associated Word: Goods (noun).

Joint Obligations (noun): This means that two or more parties share a duty or obligation under the contract.
Associated Words: Duties and Obligations (collocation), Party (noun), Under the Contract (collocation).

Obligations Under (e.g. clause 5.2) (collocation): This phrase means to refer to a particular clause or term in the contract. Lawyers in correspondence often use this term. For example, *"We refer to your client's failure to fulfil their contractual obligations under clause 7.3 of the Agreement"*. The phrase "under clause….." is a useful way to refer to a clause in a contract.
Associated Words: Clause (noun), To Fulfil (verb), Obligation (noun).

To Pass (verb): In legal English this has a similar meaning to transfer. For instance the phrase "to pass legal title" means to transfer legal title. "To pass risk" is also a common legal English phrase used in commercial contracts and means that risk is transferred from one party to another.
Associated Words: Passed (past simple), Passed (3rd form), Title (noun), Risk (noun).

Premises (noun): This is a formal and legal English word that means property or building.

Quality (noun): This means the standard of the good or service. It is usually an implied term in a commercial contract that the good or service is of a reasonable quality for the intended use.
Associated Words: Goods (noun), Implied Term (noun).

Restrictive Covenants (noun): This means that a party is forbidden or not allowed to do something stated in the contract. Restrictive covenants are usually included in employment and commercial property contracts. For example, in employment contracts there are usually confidentiality clauses that state that after an employee leaves their job, they must not release any trade secrets or confidential information about the employer. This is a type of restrictive covenant.
Associated Words: Confidentiality (noun), Party (noun).

Right of Cancellation (collocation): Some commercial contracts include a clause that allows the parties a chance to cancel the contract in certain situations. This is known as the right of cancellation.
Associated Words: Clause (noun), Party (noun).

Risk (noun): This means a chance of danger or loss. Risk is a very important concept in commercial contracts and during negotiations. Both buyers and sellers must be aware of the potential risks of entering into the contract. Due to the nature of risk in commercial contracts, parties will include warranties, indemnities, guarantees and covenants to reduce their risk.
Associated Words: To Risk (verb), Covenant (noun), To Enter Into (phrasal verb), Guarantee (noun), Indemnity (noun), To Negotiate (verb),

Warranty (noun).

Sample (noun): This is a small part, piece or an example of the goods or products for sale under a commercial contract. For example, when a shop wishes to buy an amount of fruit from a wholesaler, it is common for the shop to ask for samples of the fruit to be sent and tested before entering into a contract.
Associated Word: Goods (noun).

To be of Satisfactory Quality (collocation): This is a standard phrase in commercial contracts that means that the goods or services being provided under the contract must be of a reasonable quality and fit for the purpose of the contract.
Associated Words: Fit for Purpose (collocation), Goods (noun), Quality (noun).

Termination (noun): This means to end or finish. In legal English the word termination is used when a commercial contract comes to an end. There are many different ways of terminating a contract and each one will carry its own legal consequences. Examples of contract termination include material breach of contract, fixed-term expiration and force majeure.
Associated Words: To Terminate (verb), Terminated (past simple), Terminated (3rd form), Breach of Contract (collocation), Expiration (noun), Fixed-Term (noun), Force Majeure (noun), Material Breach (collocation).

Terms and Conditions (noun): These are the requirements and tasks to be completed under the contract. The terms and conditions section of the contract will usually be the longest part. This is where the duties and obligations of the parties are explained. It will also set out the possible consequences for not fulfilling the duties and obligations, for instance it will detail the warranties, indemnities and guarantees of the contract.
Associated Words: Clause (noun), Guarantee (noun), Indemnity (noun), Set Out (phrasal verb), Under the Contract (collocation), Warranty (noun).

Value Added Tax "VAT" (noun): This is a tax placed on goods or services which are paid for by the buyer. VAT is like a sales tax in that ultimately only the end consumer is taxed. There are strict rules and regulations in most jurisdictions that state which goods and services are

allowed to charge VAT and which are not.
Associated Words: Goods (noun), Jurisdiction (noun).

Variation (noun): This word means a change or alteration. Many commercial contracts need to be changed or altered at some point and so most agreements will include a variation clause. This allows the parties to agree the terms of variation in writing and for that change to be fully implemented into the main contract.
Associated Words: To Vary (verb), Varied (past simple), Varied (3rd form), Clause (noun), Party (noun).

Warranty (noun): This is a promise or guarantee made by a party that a fact (or facts) in a contract are true. Warranties are usually given from the seller to the buyer in relation to the quality of goods and services and legal title of goods for sale. For example, Mr Bennett wishes to buy a car from Mrs Gordon. Mr Bennett wants to be sure that the car is less than 5 years old and in reasonable condition for use. Mr Bennett will ask Mrs Gordon to include an express warranty in the contract that the car is less than 5 years old and in reasonable condition for use. Mr Bennett then decides to buy the car. If the car is not less than 5 years old or not in reasonable condition for use, Mr Bennett will be able to use this warranty if he wishes to bring a civil claim against Mrs Gordon. There are two main types of warranty. An express warranty is a warranty stated in the contract. An implied warranty is a warranty that is not stated in the contract, but can be relied on if it is reasonable to do so. For example, a common implied warranty is that the goods on sale are the same as the goods that are advertised.
Associated Words: Goods (noun), Guarantee (noun), Title (noun), Party (noun), Quality (noun).

5 BOILERPLATE CLAUSES

Applicable Law/Governing Law (noun): This means the law of the country that will govern the contract. The two phrases are very similar in meaning and only differ when used in different contexts. In a commercial contract, the phrase governing law will usually be used. The parties use this clause to state which country's laws (e.g. the laws of England and Wales) will govern the contract. Sometimes, in the event of a dispute, the phrase applicable law is used. It is important to distinguish between applicable law/governing law and jurisdiction.
Associated Words: Clause (noun), Dispute (noun), Party (noun).

Assignment (noun): This clause deals with the parties transferring the rights (and liabilities) under the contract to another party. Another term for this is Novation.
Associated Words: To Assign (verb), Clause (noun), Novation (noun).

Boilerplate Clause (noun): This is a standard clause in a commercial contract which is commonly found in most agreements. Examples of boilerplate clauses are confidentiality, force majeure, governing law and jurisdiction.
Associated Words: Clause (noun), Confidentiality (noun), Force Majeure (noun), Governing Law (noun), Jurisdiction (noun).

Confidentiality (noun): This commercial contract clause will state that the contents and information that appears in the contract and any

supplementary documents to it will remain secret and confidential between the parties. Confidentiality clauses are very common in employment contracts and usually allow for a period of time after the employee leaves the position for all confidential and secret information to not be disclosed.
Associated Word: Clause (noun).

Conflict of Laws (noun): This clause deals with the situation where there is a dispute over which laws govern the contract. Commercial contracts may contain a clause which expressly states which country's law will govern the contract and this clause is called an applicable law clause or governing law clause.
Associated Words: Applicable Law (noun), Clause (noun), Dispute (noun), Governing Law (noun).

Entire Agreement (noun): This clause states that only the clauses written in the contract are valid. All pre-contractual discussions, negotiations and representations are excluded from the contract. It is common for this clause to try to prevent any reliance on misrepresentations made before the execution of the commercial contract.
Associated Words: Clause (noun), To Execute (verb), Misrepresentation (noun), To Negotiate (verb), Valid (adjective).

Exclusion (noun): This clause attempts to restrict the rights of parties' liabilities under the contract. It is common for parties to try to prevent other parties enforcing their rights under the contract by including an exclusion of liability clause. There are statutory limitations on what types of liability can be excluded in commercial contracts.
Associated Words: Clause (noun), To Enforce (verb), Liability (noun), Rights (noun).

Exclusivity (noun): This means that one party to a commercial contract will have the exclusive right to do something (usually sell goods) in a certain geographical area or jurisdiction. Exclusivity clauses are very common in commercial contracts for goods because it provides the seller with certainty that the buyer will only sell goods provided by the seller in a specific place. The clause can also be an advantage for the buyer as the contract could include an exclusivity clause that the seller will only sell to the buyer (and no-one else) in this specific jurisdiction.

Associated Words: Goods (noun), Jurisdiction (noun).

Force Majeure (noun): This is a very common clause in commercial contracts because it states that the parties become free from their contractual duties and obligations if specific or extraordinary situations make it impossible for the parties to fulfil their obligations. Common examples that are included in a force majeure clause are wars, riots, strikes and natural disasters (also known as Acts of God).
Associated Words: Clause (noun), Duties and Obligations (collocation), To Fulfil (verb).

To Give Warranties/Indemnties/Guarantees (collocation): This collocation is used when one party provides or grants a warranty, indemnity or guarantee to another party. It is commonly used in pre-contractual negotiations and in written commercial contracts. It is the correct form to use when referring to these representations and statements in commercial contracts. For example, "Company A gave a warranty to Company B that they possessed legal title to the goods".
Associated Words: Goods (noun), Guarantee (noun), Indemnity (noun), To Negotiate (verb), Pre-Contractual (noun), Representation (noun), Title (noun), Warranty (noun).

Good Faith (noun): To act in good faith means to behave in an honest way without intending to cause any unfair influence or disadvantage onto another party. It is common in many jurisdictions that an implied term of a commercial contract is to act in good faith.
Associated Words: To Act in Good Faith (collocation), Jurisdiction (noun), Party (noun).

INCO terms (noun): Inco terms (or International Commercial Terms) are internationally recognized rules for conducting business using common commercial terms and procedures. Commercial contracts that cover different jurisdictions, especially, shipping contracts, commonly use INCO terms as their main standard terms and conditions of trade.
Associated Words: Jurisdiction (noun), Terms and Conditions (noun).

Limitation (noun): Parties can include a provision that limits the amount of damages that can be claimed in the event of a breach contract.

Alternatively, parties can also include a time limitation in the contract to state a time limit for any claims to be issued in relation to the contract.
Associated Words: Breach of Contract (collocation), Provision (noun).

Notice (noun): This means stating or notifying that something has been done or a party wishes to do something. Notice provisions in a contract usually relate to specific parts of information that must be given to another party. For example, some commercial contracts can be terminated upon notice. This means that one party states to the other that they wish to end the contract. There will usually be a notice period for this event for example, a contract may state that the notice period for terminating the contract is four weeks. This is called giving notice.
Associated Words: To Give Notice (collocation), Notice Period (noun), Provision (noun), To Terminate (verb).

Restraint of Trade (noun): This clause deals with the situation when one party tries to limit the business, trade or activity of another. Commercial contracts must be careful if a party wishes to include a restraint of trade clause as it must not conflict with anti-competition law. However, this type of clause is commonly found in employment contracts.
Associated Word: Clause (noun).

Set-off (noun): This is a provision a commercial contract where the parties agree that if a party defaults under the contract, then any money owed to the defaulting party does not have to be paid.
Associated Words: To Default (verb), To Owe (verb).

Severability (noun): This means that if a clause or section of the contract is found to be illegal or unenforceable then the other parts of the contract are still valid and will still apply. It is common for contracts to include a severability clause because usually contracts can continue to operate without the illegal clause.
Associated Words: Clause (noun), To Enforce (verb).

Void (adjective): This means that a clause, term or provision in the contract is unenforceable and has no legal effect.
Associated Words: Clause (noun), To Enforce (verb), Provision (noun), Term (noun).

6 GLOSSARY

Types of Contracts

Agency Agreement
Consumer Credit Agreement
Distance Selling
Distribution Agreement
E-commerce
Franchise
To Hire
Hire Agreement
Hire-Purchase Agreements
Insurance
Lease
To License
Loan Agreement
Marketing
Outsourcing
Sale of Goods
Subrogation
Supply of Services

Commercial Considerations

To Accept
To Affirm
To Amend
Authority to Contract
To Breach
Capacity to Contract
To Consent
Consideration
Damages
To Dispute
Duress
To Enforce
To Enter Into
To Expire
Frustration
Heads of Terms
Injunction
Intention
To Let
Liquidated Damages
Mitigation of Loss
To Negotiate
To Offer
Power of Attorney
Pre-Contractual
Privity of Contract
Remedy
To Renew
To Rent
To Rescind
Restitution
Specific Performance
To Take Instructions
Uncertainty

Unfair Contract Terms
Unsolicited Goods
Valid

Introductory Contract Terms

To Accrue
To Apply to
Business Day
By/In Instalments
To Collect From
Creditor
To be Deemed
Definitions
To Delay
Duties and Obligations
Express Terms
To Execute
Forthwith
From Time to Time
Hereunder
Implied Terms.
In Arrears
In Respect of
Joint and Several Liability
To be Made on
Neither Party
Notwithstanding/Notwithstanding the Foregoing
Outstanding
Penalty Clause
Price
To Rely On/Upon
Representations
To Set Out
Schedule
Subject to
Sums Due
To Supply
Term of Art
Thereof
Time is of the Essence
Under/At Clause

Duties and Obligations

All Reasonable Endeavours
Bill of Lading
Carriage by Sea
Charter Party
To Clear Funds
Commission
Contingent Obligations
Data Protection
To Default/To be In Default
Default Provisions
Defective Product
Description
To Discharge
Encumbrance
Fair Wear and Tear
Fit for Purpose
To be Free from
Guarantee
Indemnity
Innominate Term
In Relation to
Invoice
Joint Obligations
Liable
Obligations Under
To Pass
Premises
Quality
Restrictive Covenants
Right of Cancellation
Risk
Sample
To be of Satisfactory Quality
Termination
Terms and Conditions

Title to Goods
Trade Description
Value Added Tax "VAT"
Variation
Warranty

Boilerplate Clauses

Applicable Law/Governing Law
Assignment
Boilerplate Clause
Confidentiality
Conflict of Laws
Entire Agreement
Exclusion
Exclusivity
Force Majeure
To Give Warranties/Indemnities/Guarantees
Good Faith
INCO terms
Limitation
Notice
Restraint of Trade
Set-off
Severability
Void

Drafting Commercial Contracts

EXERCISES

7 TRUE OR FALSE

Decide if these sentences are true or false (answers are at the back of the book):

1. A distance selling contract is a contract that is entered into without the parties meeting each other face to face. Such contracts can be made over the internet or over the phone.

2. A company (A) grants a licence to another company (B) to sell, manufacture and distribute company A's products. Company B will usually use company A's method, trademarks and technology and will be paid a royalty or commission from the profit. This type of commercial contract is called a marketing agreement.

3. An agreement for the use of property or land for a fixed period of time is called a lease.

4. Under an intellectual property licence agreement, the licensor gives permission to the licensee to use its intellectual property for a period of time. Under a standard licence agreement legal title will pass from the licensor to the licensee.

5. Common examples of outsourcing agreements are for IT services, telephone call centres and basic office administration. This means that an external provider is responsible for supplying these services.

6. To alter is the correct verb to use in legal English if a commercial contract needs to be changed.

7. Consideration is required for a commercial contract to be legally binding and enforceable. Consideration means that both parties receive something as a result of the transaction. Without consideration, a commercial contract is void.

8. In legal English, the verb to enforce means that the contract (or a clause in the contract) is legal and binding and can be used or relied on in a court of law.

9. For a liquidated damages clause to be valid in a commercial contract, the amount of the damages must be a genuine pre-estimate of loss.

10. The law of rescission means that the court orders the defendant to pay any profits that resulted from their breach of contract to the claimant.

11. Any day that is not a weekend or national holiday is called a business day.

12. The section of a commercial contract where the most important terms and phrases are explained in detail to avoid misinterpretation or misunderstanding is called the recitals.

13. The verb to execute means to sign and date the contract to confirm all the parties agree to the terms and give the agreement a date.

14. In some commercial contracts a clause may state that where there is a group of two or more people who are liable for payment under a contract, all of the members of the group are liable individually and also together as a group. This is called joint and individual liability.

15. The general legal English term that means the cost or the value of the goods or service provided in the contract is the price.

16. The legal English phrase commonly found in commercial contracts that means that the goods subject to the contract are being transported by ship or boat is shipment by sea.

17. Mrs Black sells mobile phones. She receives a basic salary plus 15% of the value of every mobile phone that she sells. This 15% is called commission.

18. An encumbrance is a third party right or charge that another party may have over property or land.

19. Indemnities, warranties and guarantees are synonyms. Their meanings are the same when used in commercial contracts.

20. To pass risk is a common legal English phrase used in commercial contracts and means that risk is transferred from one party to another.

8 VOCABULARY EXERCISE

Complete the sentences with the missing word or phrase (answers are at the back of the book):

1. An _____ agreement is an arrangement between two parties where one party (the "principal") asks another party (the "agent") to represent them and create contractual legal relationships with a third party.

2. The general term for trading over the internet is called e-_____.

3. The verb commonly used in legal English which means paying money to borrow something from someone or to use a product or service temporarily is to _____.

4. There are many different types of _____ agreement and each type has very specific conditions that must be met in order for compensation to be paid for any loss suffered. Usually, the customer will pay a premium every month to be covered by a policy.

5. _____ is when a third party is given the rights or remedies of a claimant against a defendant. Under this doctrine a claimant may not claim for the same loss if they have previously transferred this right to a third party (for example, an insurance company).

6. A common remedy that is available to a party is to ask the court to _____ the contract. This means that the court makes a declaration that the contract is valid and enforceable.

7. Common phrases used in commercial contracts are "_____ of terms and conditions" or "_____ of obligations". This word means that something is broken or that a party has not done something that they should have done.

8. _____ means that a contract will be discharged because an event or situation caused the main duties and obligations of the contract to be impossible to be fulfilled.

9. The name of the remedy available from the court that states that a party must do something or stop from doing something is an _____.

10. _____ of contract means that only a party to a contract may benefit from the rights in that contract or have duties and obligations imposed upon them.

11. My contract with the bank states that *"Interest will _____ on the amount of money in arrears at a rate of 6%"*. This means that if I am late with my loan payments to the bank, they will charge extra interest on the amount of money that is late.

12. A _____ is a person or organisation who is owed money. In relation to loans, this is usually a bank.

13. If a person or company misses an instalment or a payment that they should have made, then their account will be_____. It is common for commercial contracts to contain a clause the extra interest rate will increase on this amount of money.

14. In legal English, if a contract states that ____ __ __ ___ _____ then there is a suggestion that there will be serious consequences for breaches of terms and conditions that involve time.

15. *"The seller must use ____ _____ _____ to deliver the goods within 14 days of the date of the order"*. This means that the seller must do everything that is reasonably possible to fulfil this obligation under the contract.

16. If a buyer does not pay an invoice on time then they are __ _____ __ the payment.

17. In commercial contracts, products or goods which are not of reasonable quality or not fit for their purpose are called _____ products.

18. To be legally responsible for an act or omission that causes harm or loss to another is to be _____ for that act or omission.

19. In some employment contracts there are confidentiality clauses that state that after an employee leaves their job, they must not release any trade secrets or confidential information about the employer. This type of clause is called a _____ covenant.

20. There are two main types of_____. The "express" type is stated in the contract, while the "implied" type is not stated in the contract but can be relied on if it is reasonable to do so. For example, a common example of the implied type is that the goods on sale are the same as the goods that are advertised.

9 PREPOSITION EXERCISE

Complete the sentences using the correct preposition (answers are at the back of the book):

1. A party must have authority ___ contract to enter into a legally binding contract. This means that they must have the right to sign the contract, either for themselves or for an organisation.

2. One of the most common types of commercial contracts are for the sale ___ goods or services.

3. The phrase "to enter ___" is used in commercial contracts to describe the act of agreeing to negotiate or agreeing to contract with another party.

4. If a party does not have capacity ___ contract then it is not legally binding on that party. Common examples of parties who do not have capacity to contract are children and people who are mentally impaired.

5. The document that sets out the basic terms of a contract, especially for pre-contractual negotiations is called the heads ___ terms.

6. The concept in common law that means that a person who has suffered loss must take reasonable action to stop or reduce any further loss or damage is called mitigation ___ loss.

7. If a person is not physically or mentally able to enter into a commercial contract themselves, it is possible for them to grant their solicitor or another individual a power ___ attorney. This means that a person is legally entitled to enter into contracts or agreements on behalf of someone else.

8. *"This contract for the sale of goods listed in Appendix A of this agreement applies ___ the provision of services in the European Union only".*

9. It is common for commercial contracts to attach a payment schedule to the back of the main contract if payment for the goods or services are made ___ instalments.

10. *"The buyer must collect the goods _____ the seller at the seller's address stated above within 14 days of the date of the invoice".*

11. ___ respect of is a common phrase used in commercial contracts. It is a phrase that means connected to something. For example, a clause may state "The buyer is responsible for payment of all VAT and excise duties ___ respect of the purchased goods".

12. A commercial contract will usually start with the date. Common wording for this could be *"This agreement is made ___ 28th July 2014."*

13. Your client is in breach of contract. They failed to pay for the invoices for the goods by the due date. Our client will rely ___ clause 4.7 of the contract where this is clearly stated.

14. The force majeure provisions can be found _____ clause 13 of the contract.

15. Fit ___ purpose means that the goods or services for sale is suitable for the intended use of the goods or services. This is usually an implied term of a commercial contract.

16. My client insists that the goods sold by your client are free ____ all encumbrances, defects and third party rights.

17. If a contact states that *"The guarantee given at clause 5.2 is provided ___ relation to the return or refund policy only"* then this means that the guarantee provided at clause 5.2 is connected only to the return or refund policy.

18. To be ___ satisfactory quality means that the goods or services being provided under the contract must be of a reasonable quality and fit for the purpose of the contract.

19. Commercial contracts will usually include a clause that states that the seller warrants that they have legal title ___ the goods. This means that they are the legal owner of the goods for sale and that they have the right to sell them.

20. "*All the company's directors have the required authority to execute contracts with the seller from time ___ time.*"

Drafting Commercial Contracts

10 COLLOCATION EXERCISE

Complete the sentences using the correct collocation (answers are at the back of the book):

1. A contract where a third party (for example, a financial institution) agrees to finance the purchase of goods or services is called a consumer _____ agreement.

2. Under a _____ agreement, a third party agrees to market and sell goods using their own brand name. The third party is responsible for marketing and delivering the goods to the buyer.

3. A contract between a person who pays to use a product or service for a period of time is called a _____ agreement. These contracts are commonly used for cars and other vehicles.

4. The common contract between a buyer and seller for products or things for sale is called a sale of _____ contract.

5. A standard contract for the _____ of services needs to include terms and conditions for price, inflation, third party costs, transport costs, development and improvement costs, term, termination, quality of the services to be provided, exclusivity and dispute resolution.

6. In legal English, the collocation to _____ instructions means the client will tell their lawyer what they want the lawyer to do and what to include in a contract.

7. Goods or products that are delivered to someone who has not ordered them are called _____ goods.

8. "_____ _party may use the premises between the hours of 10pm and 6am on any day"_. This means that both parties are not allowed to use the property at the stated time.

9. A common commercial contract clause is _"The parties agree to fulfil all their duties and obligations as ____ out in this agreement"_. This means that the parties agree to complete their duties, which have been stated or written in full somewhere else in the contract.

10. Industry specific terms are called terms of ____ in legal English. Examples of these in commercial contracts are force majeure, boilerplate clause, warranties and indemnities.

11. A bill of _____ is a document used in shipping contracts. It is usually in the form of a receipt that the carrier of the goods (the ship) will give to the seller (or the agent of the seller) as evidence that the goods have been loaded and are being transported to the buyer. It is a legally binding document and can confirm the fulfilment of a contractual obligation.

12. To _____ funds is the legal English phrase that means payment for the goods or services safely arrives in the bank account of the seller.

13. If a product becomes dirty, marked, scratched or damaged during its natural life, then there may be provisions in the contract that deal with fair wear and _____.

14. Commercial contracts usually include a clause that allows the parties a chance to cancel the contract in certain situations. This is known as the _____ of cancellation.

15. A _____ agreement is a contract where the debtor will borrow money from the creditor and agrees to pay the money back, usually in instalments, plus interest for an agreed period of time.

16. A tax placed on goods or services which are paid for by the final consumer or buyer is known as VAT. Its full name is value _____ tax.

17. The collocation used in legal English when one party provides or grants a warranty, indemnity or guarantee to another party is to _____ a warrant, indemnity or guarantee.

18. If a party tries to limit the business, trade or activity of another, then this clause is called a _____ of trade clause.

19. A set-___ provision in a commercial contract is where the parties agree that if a party defaults under the contract, then any money owed to the defaulting party does not have to be paid.

20. An agreement where a hirer has the option to buy the goods after a period of time, or after a certain amount of the loan has been re-paid is called a hire-_____ agreement.

11 REPLACE THE INCORRECT WORD

Find and replace the incorrect word with the correct one (answers are at the back of the book):

1. To affirm means to allow or to permit something to be done or to happen.

2. The legal English word for compensation or money paid by the liable party to the successful party is 'interest'.

3. The term "under pressure" means that a person is being forced to do something that they do not want to do. In a legal English context it means that someone is forcing a party to sign or execute a contract that they do not want to sign.

4. The legal English term that means two or more parties discuss their positions with a view to agreeing a settlement, agreement or a contract is to accept.

5. There are three main types of solution in commercial contract disputes. The most common is damages, the second main type are equitable, such as an injunction or specific performance and the third main type are declaratory judgments.

6. The principle of the remedy called restitution is to put all the parties back in the position they were in before they entered into the contract.

7. Clause 3.5 of the contract states *"the seller agrees to deliver the goods within 14 days of the date of the order dependent to full payment for all ordered goods having been received within 7 days of the date of the order"*.

8. Commercial contracts will usually state an exact date when payment must be made. This means that all sums owed by this date must be paid in full.

9. If the standard terms of a commercial contract do not vary, change or alter, then these provisions can be referred to as original provisions.

10. Once a contract is terminated and the parties are free of their contractual obligations, then it is said that the parties are excused from the contract.

11. An innominate term is a formal promise made that is intended to be relied upon. A commercial contract will contain a number of these, for instance, if the goods are defective then the seller will refund the buyer.

12. The document used to detail the products, goods or services that have been ordered by the buyer is called a bill of lading.

13. Buyers and sellers must be aware of the potential remedies of entering into the contract. Accordingly, parties will include warranties, indemnities, guarantees and covenants.

14. Many commercial contracts need to be changed or altered at some point and so most agreements will include an amendment clause. This allows the parties to agree the terms of any changes in writing.

15. Examples of restrictive covenants are force majeure, severability, governing law and jurisdiction clauses.

16. Clause 17.2 states *"The contents of this agreement together with all supplementary documents will remain exclusive between the parties"*.

17. Severability clauses are very common in commercial contracts for goods because, for example, it provides the seller with certainty that the buyer will only sell the goods provided by the seller in a specific place.

18. The parties may wish to include a provision that restricts the amount of damages that can be claimed in the event of a breach contract. This type of clause is called an exclusion clause.

19. A clause, term or provision in the contract that is ruled unenforceable by the court and has no legal effect is called a penalty clause.

20. Civil litigation claims are also commonly called disagreements.

12 ANSWERS

True or False:

1. True

2. False

3. True

4. False

5. True

6. False

7. True

8. True

9. True

10. False

11. True

12. False

13. True

14. False

15. True

16. False

17. True

18. True

19. False

20. True

Vocabulary Exercise:

1. agency

2. commerce

3. hire/rent

4. insurance

5. Subrogation

6. affirm

7. breach

8. Frustration

9. injunction

10. Privity

11. accrue

12. creditor

13. in arrears

14. time is of the essence

15. all reasonable endeavours

16. in default of

17. defective

18. liable

19. restrictive

20. warranty

Drafting Commercial Contracts

Prepositions Exercise:

1. to

2. of

3. into

4. to

5. of

6. of

7. of

8. to

9. in/by

10. from

11. In

12. on

13. on/upon

14. under/at

15. for

16. from

17. in

18. of

19. to

20. to

Collocations Exercise:

1. credit

2. distribution

3. hire

4. goods

5. supply

6. take

7. unsolicited

8. Neither

9. set

10. art

11. lading

12. clear

13. tear

14. right

15. loan

16. added

17. give

18. restraint

19. off

20. purchase

Drafting Commercial Contracts

Replace the Incorrect Word

1. ~~affirm~~, consent

2. ~~interest~~, damages

3. ~~pressure~~, duress

4. ~~accept~~, negotiate

5. ~~solution~~, remedy

6. ~~restitution~~, rescission

7. ~~dependent~~, subject

8. ~~owed~~, due

9. ~~original~~, default

10. ~~excused~~, discharged

11. ~~innominate term~~, guarantee

12. ~~bill of lading~~, invoice

13. ~~remedies~~, risks

14. ~~amendment~~, variation

15. ~~restrictive covenants~~, boilerplate clauses

16. ~~exclusive~~, confidential

17. ~~severability~~, exclusivity

18. ~~exclusion~~, limitation

19. ~~penalty~~, void

20. ~~disagreements~~, disputes

ABOUT THE AUTHOR

Michael Howard is a solicitor and legal English lecturer from London. He grew up in Surrey, England and qualified as a solicitor in 2005. After many years of legal practice he decided to go on an adventure around Europe and the Middle East lecturing law and teaching English. His travels took him to Poland, Germany, Dubai, Abu Dhabi and finally back to the UK where he was invited to teach legal English to foreign lawyers and law students at courses run at Cambridge University. Michael now works in legal publishing and spends his free time writing vocabulary and study packs to help foreign lawyers improve their legal English. In April 2013 he published his first set of books on the English Legal System and in November 2013 he followed this up with Civil Litigation and Dispute Resolution. The most recent set in his catalogue is entitled Drafting Commercial Contracts. Alongside writing and publishing he spends time with his family and friends in South London and playing the guitar. His dictionaries and exercise books are all available on Amazon on Kindle and in paperback.

Legal Disclaimer: This book contains information on the vocabulary used by lawyers to draft commercial contracts. It is written for the benefit of lawyers and law students whose first language is not English. The information is not advice, and should not be treated as such. You must not rely on the information in the book as an alternative to legal, financial, taxation, or accountancy advice from an appropriately qualified professional. If you have any specific questions about any legal, financial, or accountancy matters you should consult an appropriately qualified professional. We do not represent, warrant, undertake or guarantee that the information in the book is correct, accurate, complete or non-misleading and that the use of the guidance in the book will lead to any particular outcome or result.

Drafting Commercial Contracts

Printed in Great Britain
by Amazon